THE ANTI-INSOMNIA NOTEBOOK
An Evidence-Based Program for Better Sleep

A six-week guided program designed by therapists to help you improve your sleep through Cognitive Behavioral Therapy for Insomnia, the most effective, non-pharmaceutical treatment for disrupted sleep.

. . . .
(THIS BOOK BELONGS TO)

. . . .
(IF FOUND, PLEASE RETURN TO)

LEARN MORE
www.therapynotebooks.com

THERAPY NOTEBOOKS
Published by Subject Matters

ISBN: 9781958963982
Printed in the USA

LEAD THERAPISTS
Jessica Yu, PhD
Diana Hu, PsyD
Hod Tamir, PhD

EDITED BY
Anna Shults Held
Dana Hatic

DESIGNED BY
Monumento.Co

BRANDING BY
High Tide

IF YOU ARE IN
URGENT NEED OF ASSISTANCE:
Dial 9-1-1

FOR MENTAL HEALTH
CRISIS SUPPORT:
Dial 9-8-8

SAMHSA National Helpline
1-800-622-HELP (4357)

Crisis Text Line
Text HOME to 741741

This book was designed for your sleepless nights.

This six-week, guided notebook was designed to be simple, easy-to-use, and focused on teaching you foundational principles to improve your sleep. We recommend following the contents of this notebook in order, and incorporating the new concepts you learn in each subsequent week of practice.

This book is founded upon the principles of Cognitive Behavioral Therapy for Insomnia (CBT-I).

CBT-I is consistently effective in treating insomnia, and more effective than any prescription or over-the-counter sleep-aid for improving quantity and quality of sleep.[1][2] It uses the principles of Cognitive Behavioral Therapy (CBT), a form of psychological treatment based on changing unhelpful patterns of thought and behavior, to address persistent sleep issues.

Disclaimer: Some health disorders are not suited for CBT-I.[3] These include epilepsy, bipolar disorders, and those at high risk for falls. Sleep restriction can also exacerbate symptoms for those with untreated disorders of excessive sleepiness and with parasomnias. If you are feeling drowsy to the extent where you are putting yourself in danger, discontinue your CBT-I practice immediately and contact your physician.

Our hope: to empower you with tools and strategies to improve your sleep.

Program Overview

Over the next six weeks, you will keep a daily sleep log. Each week, you will establish and adjust your weekly sleep schedule. This work is the core of sleep change. You will also learn about stimulus control, sleep hygiene, and cognitive reframing as additional tools that set a solid foundation for sleep.

PROGRAM	TOOL	PURPOSE
Week I:	Sleep Log	Take stock of your sleep patterns
Week II:	Sleep Restriction	Adjust your schedule to improve sleep drive
Week III:	Stimulus Control	Create associations between "bed" and "sleep"
Week IV:	Sleep Hygiene	Learn healthy habits to improve sleep quality
Week V:	Cognitive Reframing	Reframe thought patterns to reduce sleep anxiety
Week VI:	Relapse Prevention	Create a plan to recognize and respond to future sleep struggles

Letter From
a Therapist

First of all, we want to express how humbled we are that you chose to pick up this book. Working on your sleep requires perseverance and grit, and we're honored to be on this journey with you. Second of all, let's talk about why you're here. As much as "sleep" can conjure images of peace, comfort, and ease, it's also a word that can be associated with a sense of anxiety, and a gnawing desperation for rest.

If you are reading this letter because you are one of the many that experience sleep as anything but restful, you are not alone. Each year, approximately 30 to 40% of adults in the United States report symptoms of insomnia—this can look like difficulty falling asleep, difficulty staying asleep, and feeling drowsy or fatigued during the day.[4] Their sleep problems extend beyond difficulty sleeping, and commonly include changes in mood, difficulty concentrating, and difficulty performing at work or school. As a result, many of these adults seek help for their sleep problems, trying everything from over-the-counter sleep aids, to meditation and mindfulness, to seeking advice from their doctors.

As clinical psychologists who have spent the last decade working in primary care clinics, large hospital systems, and private practice, we have met many of these individuals. And we can confidently say that if you are one of the millions of Americans who is looking for help with your sleep, you're in the right place.

There is one treatment in practice that has proven to be more effective than any other: Cognitive Behavioral Therapy for Insomnia, or CBT-I.[5] It is a treatment that does not involve any medications or special devices. Rather, it is a process that empowers you with the knowledge and skill to take a close look at how you sleep and build a repertoire of healthy habits and strategies to improve your sleep quality and quantity. In creating this journal, we sought to put that knowledge and skill into your hands. Now, before you turn the page, let us say—we applaud you. It takes effort and openness to look at a problem, seek help, and try something new.

Even taking this first step is something to be proud of. It takes even more effort when you're not sleeping well. Be mindful that this journal will not change your sleep overnight. You'll have to learn about the skills, implement them in your daily life, and make adjustments as your sleep begins to change. You've taken the first step by being here—and we'll be guiding you every step of the way.

Sincerely,

Jessica Yu, PhD & Diana Hu, PsyD
Lead Clinicians

Scan the QR code to
meet our clinicians

How This Book Helps You

1   Practice the most effective non-pharmaceutical program
        for sleepless nights: Cognitive Behavioral Therapy for Insomnia.

        By challenging attitudes that might contribute to sleeplessness, you
        can increase your chances of a better night's rest. We designed this
        6-week program to help you sustainably improve your sleep quantity
        and quality.

2   Transform your sleep by identifying your patterns.

        If you struggle with sleep, you know the frustration of being stuck
        in an endless, self-perpetuating loop. We'll help you find relief by
        tracking your daily sleep patterns to make healthy, sustainable
        adjustments.

3   Discover the science of sleep.

        Sleep is vital to human development, and helps your brain process
        the events of the day. In these pages, you'll learn the foundational
        research and principles of sleep that will empower you to achieve
        lasting, quality rest.

4   Improve your sleep hygiene with research-backed tools
        and strategies.

        Our modern world makes it difficult to wind down and switch off.
        We'll help you identify ways you can change your behaviors and your
        environment to experience optimal sleep.

5   Made by therapists with experience in clinics, hospitals,
        and private practice.

        We worked with therapists who deeply understand the impact
        of insomnia on quality of life. They'll guide you with tips and
        reminders along your journey that actually help.

Contents

I INTRODUCTION:
On Insomnia

Fatigue is painful. Physically, mentally, and emotionally, persistent tiredness can make us feel less equipped to handle daily life. We may have trouble mustering the energy for social activities, lose focus at work, or find ourselves being impatient with our family. And no matter how exhausted we are, the relief of sleep may feel impossibly far away.

Like eating, transportation, and communication, the way we sleep has changed throughout human history. But as long as we've slept, we've had trouble sleeping.[6] Some believe industrialization and modern technology have made sleeping problems worse. Sleep loss and sleep issues have recently been declared public health epidemics by the American Centers for Disease Control and global World Health Organization. In the United States, we commonly dismiss being sleep deprived as a way of life.

Sleep struggles can be frustrating. The solution feels as if it should be simple—after all, we are made to sleep—but sleep is complex, with a myriad of factors contributing to good or poor sleep. It's also highly individual. Cultural factors, genetics, and lifestyle all impact sleep. As a people, we have been trying to develop solutions for centuries. Ancient remedies used herbs to address sleep deprivation. The Greeks had a god of sleep, Hypnos, to aid them. Since the early twentieth century, insomniacs have depended on medication, supplements, and alcohol, which are actually proven to reduce sleep quality.

Sleep research, while a relatively new field, has given us new insight into sleep, and new therapies to address sleep issues. The most promising method is Cognitive Behavioral Therapy for Insomnia (CBT-I). CBT-I is an evidence-based solution that addresses sleep issues by changing the mindset and patterns of behaviors around sleep. After weeks or months of sleepless nights, a good night's sleep may feel hopeless. Through CBT-I, you will be equipped with a sustainable solution that gives you the tools to sleep better.

WHY WE SLEEP

Sleep is an opportunity for your brain and body to recover from the stressors of the day. Your cells repair themselves and hormones release to support bone and muscle growth, appetite, and stress response. In the brain, sleep allows neurons to reorganize, converting short-term memories into long-term ones and clearing out waste from your nervous system so it works better when you're awake.

Your mental health is supported by two types of sleep, but in slightly different ways. Non-rapid eye movement (NREM) sleep is theorized to be like your recovery time, with this phase affecting executive functioning and stress response. Rapid eye movement (REM) sleep is the magical state of dreaming. During REM, your brain is as active as it is when you're awake, but there is almost no noradrenaline—a chemical related to stress and arousal—released. Some hypothesize REM may be a space for safe emotional processing, with your brain testing and forming new, maybe safer-feeling connections.[7][8]

Due to the nature of sleep research, we mostly define what sleep does for us by understanding what is lost when we don't sleep well. There are clear, significant links between poor sleep and nearly every health metric, such as higher mortality and higher risk of hypertension, cardiovascular disease, and diabetes. Sleep issues and insomnia are highly comorbid with many significant mental health issues, such as anxiety, depression, and PTSD.[9-13] Sleep deficits can look like someone struggling with low mood, anxiety, mood fluctuations, difficulties paying attention or organizing tasks, disproportionate reactions, irritability, and even hallucinations. And, because sleep problems are correlated with every major mental health disorder, it can be difficult to assess whether poor sleep is a cause or a symptom. Regardless, treating sleep is likely to improve other conditions.

Simply put, we aren't being unproductive when we sleep. We're doing important work for our brains and bodies.

HOW SLEEP WORKS

There are two primary factors that determine when we sleep: our circadian rhythm and sleep pressure. The circadian rhythm is a relatively precise internal clock that regulates sleep, as well as many other functions of the body like hunger. Our internal clock is set by inputs: primarily daylight, but also food, exercise, and even social interactions. Our circadian rhythms maintain our sleep cycles through melatonin release. The body releases more melatonin and begins to drop body temperature when our internal clock signals the beginning of a sleep cycle.

The second factor is sleep pressure. Sleep pressure is a buildup of adenosine, a chemical that accumulates as we are awake. When adenosine levels peak, brain cells fire more slowly, and you'll feel a greater desire to go to bed. For most people, this is 12 to 16 hours after waking. If you get inadequate sleep, you build up a "sleep debt" of residual adenosine from the night before, increasing your levels of tiredness while you're awake.

Your circadian rhythm and sleep pressure form your sleep drive, or your desire to sleep. The two processes operate independently of each other—your circadian rhythm marches on regardless of whether you sleep or not, while your adenosine levels continue to build over your waking periods and purge during sleep—but are typically aligned.

Once you fall asleep, you experience sleep in four stages: three NREM and one REM.

Stage 1, NREM: The transition period between wakefulness and sleep. *Heart rate, breathing, and eye movements will start to slow. Muscles start to relax.*

Stage 2, NREM: Progressing to deeper sleep. *Heart rate and breathing will continue to slow. Body temperature begins to drop.*

Stage 3, NREM: Slow wave sleep. *Eyes and muscles become completely relaxed. Heart rates, breathing, and brain waves are at their lowest levels.*

Stage 4, REM: Dream state. *Brain waves are active. Eyes move, and breath and heart rates increase.*

Each sleep cycle takes between ninety minutes and two hours. In seven to nine hours of sleep, you'll experience four or five sleep cycles. Each sleep cycle is not created equal: NREM sleep is dominant for sleep cycles earlier in the night, whereas REM stages become longer in the later cycles. As a general rule, quality sleep follows this predictable pattern.

WHAT FACTORS DETERMINE GOOD OR BAD SLEEP?

Sleep, including the causes and effects of good and poor sleep, is highly complex. Some factors are difficult or impossible to change, like your genetics. Every human's sleep-wake cycle is between 24 and 28 hours in length. Specific waking and sleeping hours, however, vary from person to person. Researchers have found biological differences between night owls and morning larks. Evolutionarily, this is likely because we took shifts watching for threats. In the modern day, however, our society is biased toward early wakeups. The rigidity of schedules for responsibilities like school and work can make getting adequate sleep more difficult for some people than others. If you struggle to fall asleep or wake up at a certain time, it's likely not just a problem of willpower but also genetics. Your need for sleep, too, will vary based on demographic heuristics like age and socio-economic status. Environmental factors, like seasons and the weather, can also impact sleep.[14]

These fixed factors predispose our vulnerability to sleep problems. Precipitating incidents like a period of acute stress, a big life change like a move or new baby, or a health issue can then push us into a period of chronic sleep deprivation or insomnia. Both chronic sleep deprivation and insomnia are characterized by not getting the quality or amount of sleep you need, but they have different root causes. Sleep deprivation is a result of not giving yourself enough time to sleep, whereas insomnia is not. Clinical insomnia is defined as recurring difficulty sleeping at least three nights a week for a month. Whether you meet the clinical definition for insomnia or not, addressing behaviors and thought patterns around sleep through CBT-I can help you sleep better.

Like most major mental health disorders, sleep loss can worsen itself over time. When we can't fall asleep, we often turn to tools like alcohol, sleeping pills, or screen time to quiet our brains. Alcohol and sleeping pills can help with the onset of sleep, but their sedative qualities can alter the balance of NREM and REM sleep, decreasing the quality of sleep. Screentime, on the other hand, can make it harder to fall asleep. Our brains interpret screens' blue light as daylight, which can disrupt our circadian rhythm and delay the release of melatonin.

Then, in the morning, we use caffeine to get ourselves awake and alert. Caffeine works by blocking adenosine receptors and stimulating adrenaline production, helping you feel less tired and more alert. When you're suffering from sleep loss, this can feel like exactly what you need. However, caffeine stays in our systems long after we feel its effects, and use during the middle of day or later can make it difficult to fall asleep.

These maladaptive behaviors can turn sleep loss into a cyclical, progressive problem. We drink caffeine to stay awake, then use a depressive substance to mitigate the effects of caffeine, or screens to quiet our thoughts, which impacts our sleep quality, making us more likely to reach for caffeine, and so on.

Sleep is often thought of as a natural result of exhaustion: we sleep when we can't stay awake any longer. In actuality, sleep is an activity for which we can prepare and set goals. By creating better thought patterns around sleep and improving sleep habits, we have an opportunity to break the cycle.

WHAT IS CBT-I?

Cognitive Behavioral Therapy (CBT) is a form of psychological treatment focused on changing patterns of thoughts and behaviors. CBT has proven to be effective in addressing depression, anxiety, PTSD, and other major mental health disorders. Cognitive Behavioral Therapy for insomnia (CBT-I) was developed and refined over the last several decades thanks to an increased understanding of the biology of sleep, and the relationship between stress and arousal and sleep. Treatment typically lasts six weeks and works to increase sleep drive at the appropriate moments to improve your sleep quality and quantity, and to give you the skills to actually rest while you're in bed. CBT-I works through adjusting behavior and mindset, employing specific strategies like sleep hygiene, stimulus control, and cognitive reframing. Each week will cover a new concept to aid you in sleeping better.

We realize that CBT-I will ask a lot from you. Change can be uncomfortable, especially when it requires breaking habits and deconstructing coping mechanisms. These evidence-based exercises are not a magic fix and will not improve your sleep overnight. Rather, they are skills and tools to implement, practice, and master over time. It is important to keep in mind that this is not a zero-sum game and change is not linear. There will be good days and bad. But, if you are able to commit to the process, you will see meaningful improvement not only in your sleep, but your mood, attention and focus, outlook, and overall quality of life.

Note From
a Therapist

Before getting started with the concepts and exercises in this book, there are some foundational aspects of your mental health to keep in mind.

Sleep struggles are not one-size-fits-all, and starting a guided program like this may be intimidating. You may even have self-judgments around doing the steps of this notebook "exactly right." Keep in mind that the goal is to improve your sleep quantity and quality, not complete the program perfectly. Do the best you can to stick to the sleep logs and sleep schedule, but know that there is flexibility, and that you are in the process of finding what works for you.

Note that certain mental health conditions, such as depression, anxiety, attention-deficit/hyperactivity disorder, and post-traumatic stress disorder, can make insomnia worse. Similarly, certain neurological disorders and physical health problems, such as dementia, diabetes, chronic pain, and obstructive sleep apnea, can increase the risk of insomnia. If you have been diagnosed with one of these conditions or believe you have symptoms of one of these conditions, please consult with your medical provider as you use this journal to ensure that you get treatment for these exacerbating factors.

Finally, as you're focusing on your sleep, don't lose sight of all the other things that are important for your mental health. People with sleep difficulties are often so tired that they don't feel the energy or motivation to do much. This can take a toll on your mood. Remember to still care for yourself well: eat well, exercise, and do fun and meaningful things (you can find more recommendations in Appendix C).

WEEK I:
The Sleep Log

Note From a Therapist

The Sleep Log is the crux of CBT-I. Evaluating your sleep daily helps build awareness and insight into your daily sleep patterns. We're naturally inclined to recall the nights we slept poorly, but understanding the nights we slept well is just as important. The Sleep Log will allow you to look at your sleep with greater clarity. You will objectively measure how much you've been sleeping versus lying in bed awake, notice whether there's any regularity in your sleep pattern, and analyze how rested or not you feel each day. That clarity will help you figure out exactly how to adjust your sleep patterns.

We're asking you to fill out the Sleep Log every day for the next six weeks. Changing your sleep requires you to detect patterns in your sleep—and you can only detect patterns if you have sufficient data. More importantly, filling out the log everyday will give you a visible, tangible way of assessing how your sleep has improved over time.

To that end, we recommend completing the previous night's log first thing the next morning to increase the chances that you remember to do so. We suggest keeping this book and a pencil or pen near your bed or nightstand so that it's there for you when you wake up. Be as accurate and specific as possible, but don't worry about accuracy at the expense of relaxation.

On the following pages, you'll find a set of instructions and an example of the Sleep Log you'll be completing each night. Feel free to reference back to this section as frequently as you'd like throughout the next few weeks. After each week of data collection, you'll learn how to use your log to set a new sleep schedule that will maximize your chances of restful sleep. In addition, you will build a repertoire of accompanying strategies to help you wind down at night, ensure that your environment is conducive to sleep, and keep anxious and intrusive thoughts at bay.

Question	Instructions
1	What time did you get into bed?	This refers to the time you physically got into bed, not the time you actually fell asleep. For example, you may have started lying in bed around 10pm, but tossed and turned for an hour unable to fall asleep.
2	What time did you fall asleep?	This refers to the time you actually fell asleep. This can be really difficult to know for certain, but do your best to estimate.
3	How long were you up in the middle of the night?	This refers to the total length of time you were awake in the middle of the night. For example, you may have woken up twice and couldn't fall back asleep for about 15 minutes each.
4	What time did you finally wake up?	This refers to the time you woke up in the morning, not the time you physically got out of bed. For example, you were awake at 6 AM and didn't fall asleep again.
5	What time did you finally get out of bed?	This refers to the time you physically got out of bed after waking up.
6	Total time in bed for the night	This is how long you spent in bed the previous night. Calculate the difference between when you first got into bed (Question 1) and when you got out of bed (Question 5).

Question	Instructions
7 Total time asleep for the night	This is how long you were actually asleep. Take the difference between when you actually fell asleep (Question 2) and finally woke up for the morning (Question 4), then subtract any time you spent awake in the middle of the night (Question 3). In other words: [What time did you finally get up?] - [What time did you fall asleep?] - [About how long were you up in the middle of the night?]
8 Sleep efficiency for the night	This is measured by dividing your total time actually asleep (Question 7) by your total time in bed (Question 6): [Total time asleep for the night] / [Total time in bed for the night]
9 How would you rate your quality of sleep for the night?	This is your subjective rating of how well you slept. Circle the rating that best describes the quality of your sleep (Great, Good, Fair, or Poor).
10 How long did you doze or nap during the day yesterday?	This is how long you napped during your waking hours.
11 Additional Notes	This is a space for you to reflect on the new tools and strategies that you learn each week, and how they've impacted your sleep.

You can also jot down notes about anything that might have affected your sleep negatively—like illness, stressful situations, food or medications, etc. |

EXAMPLE:
Sleep Log Entry

Charlie got in bed at 10pm, and lied awake trying to sleep. He believes it took about an hour to finally get to sleep, around 11pm. He woke up twice in the middle of the night to use the bathroom, and took about 15 minutes to get back asleep each time. He woke up again at around 6am, did not fall back asleep, and got out of bed at 6:30am.

1   What time did you get into bed?   10:00 PM

2   What time did you fall asleep?   11:00 PM

3   How long were you up in the
     middle of the night?   30 minutes

4   What time did you finally wake up?   6:00 AM

5   What time did you finally get out
     of bed?   6:30 AM

6   Total time in bed for the night   6:30 AM - 10:00 PM = 8.5 hours

7   Total time asleep for the night   6:00 AM - 11:00 PM - 30 min = 6.5 hours

8   Sleep efficiency for the night   6.5 hours / 8.5 hours = 76%

9   How would you rate your quality   Great   (Good)   Fair   Poor
     of sleep for the night?

10   How long did you doze or nap
     during the day yesterday?   30 minutes

11   Additional Notes   Couldn't get to sleep after I got into
                                                        bed, so I took a Unisom.

NOTE FROM A THERAPIST

These notes will provide additional guidance,
tips, questions as you learn tools and strategies for
improving your sleep.

WEEK I:
Your Sleep Log Entries

WEEKLY SLEEP GOAL	
WAKE TIME	
BEDTIME	

1   What time did you get into bed?

2   What time did you fall asleep?

3   How long were you up in the
        middle of the night?

4   What time did you finally wake up?

5   What time did you finally get out
        of bed?

6   Total time in bed for the night

7   Total time asleep for the night

8   Sleep efficiency for the night

9   How would you rate your quality
        of sleep for the night?   Great   Good   Fair   Poor

10   How long did you doze or nap
        during the day yesterday?

11   Additional Notes

NOTE FROM A THERAPIST

You did it! You've completed your first sleep log and
taken your first concrete step towards better sleep.

1   What time did you get into bed?

2   What time did you fall asleep?

3   How long were you up in the middle of the night?

4   What time did you finally wake up?

5   What time did you finally get out of bed?

6   Total time in bed for the night

7   Total time asleep for the night

8   Sleep efficiency for the night

9   How would you rate your quality of sleep for the night?   Great   Good   Fair   Poor

10   How long did you doze or nap during the day yesterday?

11   Additional Notes

NOTE FROM A THERAPIST

Remember to keep this journal handy to log your sleep in the morning.

1   What time did you get into bed?

2   What time did you fall asleep?

3   How long were you up in the middle of the night?

4   What time did you finally wake up?

5   What time did you finally get out of bed?

6   Total time in bed for the night

7   Total time asleep for the night

8   Sleep efficiency for the night

9   How would you rate your quality of sleep for the night?   Great   Good   Fair   Poor

10   How long did you doze or nap during the day yesterday?

11   Additional Notes

NOTE FROM A THERAPIST

You're almost halfway through your first week of sleep logging. Do you notice any patterns emerging?

1   What time did you get into bed?

2   What time did you fall asleep?

3   How long were you up in the
        middle of the night?

4   What time did you finally wake up?

5   What time did you finally get out
        of bed?

6   Total time in bed for the night

7   Total time asleep for the night

8   Sleep efficiency for the night

9   How would you rate your quality   Great   Good   Fair   Poor
        of sleep for the night?

10   How long did you doze or nap
        during the day yesterday?

11   Additional Notes

NOTE FROM A THERAPIST

Keep going! You're collecting data that will help
you implement the tools and strategies to improve
your sleep.

1   What time did you get into bed?

2   What time did you fall asleep?

3   How long were you up in the
           middle of the night?

4   What time did you finally wake up?

5   What time did you finally get out
           of bed?

6   Total time in bed for the night

7   Total time asleep for the night

8   Sleep efficiency for the night

9   How would you rate your quality
           of sleep for the night?   Great   Good   Fair   Poor

10   How long did you doze or nap
           during the day yesterday?

11   Additional Notes

NOTE FROM A THERAPIST

If you've missed a day or two of logging this week,
be kind to yourself. Simply commit to logging for
the rest of the week.

1   What time did you get into bed?

2   What time did you fall asleep?

3   How long were you up in the
middle of the night?

4   What time did you finally wake up?

5   What time did you finally get out
of bed?

6   Total time in bed for the night

7   Total time asleep for the night

8   Sleep efficiency for the night

9   How would you rate your quality   Great   Good   Fair   Poor
of sleep for the night?

10   How long did you doze or nap
during the day yesterday?

11   Additional Notes

NOTE FROM A THERAPIST

You're nearly there! One more day of sleep logging
and you'll have a week's worth of data to digest.

1   What time did you get into bed?

. . . .

2   What time did you fall asleep?

. . . .

3   How long were you up in the
           middle of the night?

. . . .

4   What time did you finally wake up?

. . . .

5   What time did you finally get out
           of bed?

. . . .

6   Total time in bed for the night

. . . .

7   Total time asleep for the night

. . . .

8   Sleep efficiency for the night

. . . .

9   How would you rate your quality   Great   Good   Fair   Poor
           of sleep for the night?

. . . .

10   How long did you doze or nap
           during the day yesterday?

. . . .

11   Additional Notes

. . . .

. . . .

. . . .

. . . .

. . . .

. . . .

NOTE FROM A THERAPIST

Congratulations! You made it through Week 1 of
sleep logging. You're ready to set concrete goals for
your sleep.

Calculate Your
Goals for Week II

Congratulations–you've completed your first week of sleep logging.

For many with insomnia, the struggle is such that they don't have a consistent sleep routine or schedule. But without these internal and external cues, our brains and bodies don't know when it is time to rest and when it is time to wake.

In this section, you'll calculate your target bedtime and wake time for the upcoming week. We'll break it down and walk through the steps this time, and then provide a table for you to work through in the following weeks. Feel free to come back to these instructions as needed.

1   TAKE STOCK OF YOUR SLEEP

Start by referencing your sleep logs from the past week, filling in
the Total Time Asleep for each night and calculating the average:

WEEK 1: AVERAGE TIME ASLEEP									
NIGHT	1	2	3	4	5	6	7	TOTAL	AVERAGE (TOTAL ÷ 7)
TOTAL TIME ASLEEP									

Next, calculate your Average Sleep Efficiency:

WEEK 1: AVERAGE SLEEP EFFICIENCY									
NIGHT	1	2	3	4	5	6	7	TOTAL	AVERAGE (TOTAL ÷ 7)
SLEEP EFFICIENCY									

2   ADJUST YOUR SLEEP SCHEDULE

I.   *Set your wake time.*
Based on your schedule and your wake time from the past
week (considering when you need to be ready for your daily
commitments) what time do you want to be out of bed?

WAKE TIME	

II.   *Calculate your Allowable Time in Bed.*
This is the maximum amount of time you should physically be
in bed. Select the guideline that applies to your Average Sleep
Efficiency from Week 1.

If your Average Sleep Efficiency last week was over 85% and you
felt your sleep quality was good, you can allot up to 15 minutes of
extra time in bed.

If your Average Sleep Efficiency was under 85%, or if you felt that you had poor quality of sleep, then you'll keep your Allowable Time in Bed to reflect your Average Total Time Asleep.

AVERAGE TOTAL TIME ASLEEP		
AVERAGE SLEEP EFFICIENCY	◯ OVER 85%	◯ UNDER 85%
ALLOWABLE TIME IN BED		

III.   *Set your bedtime.*

Working backwards from the wake time you set, calculate when you'd need to go to bed in order to achieve the Allowable Time in Bed.

WAKE TIME	
SUBSTRACT ALLOWABLE TIME IN BED	
BEDTIME	

3   COMMIT TO YOUR SLEEP SCHEDULE

For the upcoming week, you'll want to stick with your new bedtime and wake time in order to reduce the time you spend tossing and turning in bed. Write the wake time and bedtime you just set at the beginning of next week's sleep log as a reminder.

WEEK II:
Sleep Restriction

Note From
a Therapist

If you slept poorly, you'd naturally feel inclined to "make up" for it the next night by going to bed earlier. However, the more that you lie in bed awake, the more this interrupts your sleep patterns and teaches your brain it's okay to be awake in bed.

Sleep restriction increases the ratio of sleep you get during the time you're in bed (what we call sleep efficiency). It does this by limiting the amount of time you spend in bed to more closely reflect how much you sleep. In sleep restriction, you're gradually working toward sleeping for nearly all the time you currently spend in bed.

At the end of last week, you established your bedtime and wake time for this upcoming week. You'll also refrain from taking naps during the day or spending time in bed outside of your bedtime. Doing this will help you feel sleepier and more ready to snooze once you lie down (what we call *sleep drive*), and spend more of your time in bed actually sleeping (or *sleep efficiency*).

For the first week or two of implementing your new sleep schedule, you may feel particularly tired. We know that it will be difficult to maintain, but avoiding naps and sticking to your set bed and wake times will strengthen your sleep drive, which, in turn, will help you fall asleep faster and strengthen the association between "bed" and "sleep."

Make sure to commit to your new bedtime and wake times using reminders and alarms, and clearing your schedule of tasks after your bedtime. You'll continue to log each night's sleep. At the end of each week, you'll look back at how the week went and establish your new bedtime and wake time.

WEEK II:
Your Sleep Log Entries

WEEKLY SLEEP GOAL	
WAKE TIME	
BEDTIME	

1   What time did you get into bed?

2   What time did you fall asleep?

3   How long were you up in the
       middle of the night?

4   What time did you finally wake up?

5   What time did you finally get out
       of bed?

6   Total time in bed for the night

7   Total time asleep for the night

8   Sleep efficiency for the night

9   How would you rate your quality   Great   Good   Fair   Poor
       of sleep for the night?

10   How long did you doze or nap
       during the day yesterday?

11   Additional Notes

NOTE FROM A THERAPIST

The first day of sleep restriction can be the hardest.
Recognize your resilience for committing to a new
bedtime and wake time.

1   What time did you get into bed?

2   What time did you fall asleep?

3   How long were you up in the
    middle of the night?

4   What time did you finally wake up?

5   What time did you finally get out
    of bed?

6   Total time in bed for the night

7   Total time asleep for the night

8   Sleep efficiency for the night

9   How would you rate your quality   Great   Good   Fair   Poor
    of sleep for the night?

10 How long did you doze or nap
    during the day yesterday?

11 Additional Notes

NOTE FROM A THERAPIST

Give yourself kudos for implementing the steps to
improve your sleep, especially if you're feeling tired.

1   What time did you get into bed?

2   What time did you fall asleep?

3   How long were you up in the middle of the night?

4   What time did you finally wake up?

5   What time did you finally get out of bed?

6   Total time in bed for the night

7   Total time asleep for the night

8   Sleep efficiency for the night

9   How would you rate your quality of sleep for the night?   Great   Good   Fair   Poor

10   How long did you doze or nap during the day yesterday?

11   Additional Notes

NOTE FROM A THERAPIST

Remember that sleep restriction is geared towards increasing the likelihood that when you're in bed, you're actually sleeping.

1   What time did you get into bed?

2   What time did you fall asleep?

3   How long were you up in the
        middle of the night?

4   What time did you finally wake up?

5   What time did you finally get out
        of bed?

6   Total time in bed for the night

7   Total time asleep for the night

8   Sleep efficiency for the night

9   How would you rate your quality   Great   Good   Fair   Poor
        of sleep for the night?

10   How long did you doze or nap
        during the day yesterday?

11   Additional Notes

NOTE FROM A THERAPIST

Do your best to avoid taking extra caffeine or naps.
We want your tiredness to help you fall asleep as
soon as you lie down.

1   What time did you get into bed?

2   What time did you fall asleep?

3   How long were you up in the
         middle of the night?

4   What time did you finally wake up?

5   What time did you finally get out
         of bed?

6   Total time in bed for the night

7   Total time asleep for the night

8   Sleep efficiency for the night

9   How would you rate your quality   Great   Good   Fair   Poor
         of sleep for the night?

10   How long did you doze or nap
         during the day yesterday?

11   Additional Notes

NOTE FROM A THERAPIST

Hold off on changing your routine mid-week. You'll
have the chance to adjust your bed and wake time
at the end of the week.

1   What time did you get into bed?

2   What time did you fall asleep?

3   How long were you up in the
middle of the night?

4   What time did you finally wake up?

5   What time did you finally get out
of bed?

6   Total time in bed for the night

7   Total time asleep for the night

8   Sleep efficiency for the night

9   How would you rate your quality   Great   Good   Fair   Poor
of sleep for the night?

10   How long did you doze or nap
during the day yesterday?

11   Additional Notes

NOTE FROM A THERAPIST

If you are running into issues with maintaining
your sleep schedule, see if you can recruit some
help from friends or a partner.

1   What time did you get into bed?

2   What time did you fall asleep?

3   How long were you up in the
middle of the night?

4   What time did you finally wake up?

5   What time did you finally get out
of bed?

6   Total time in bed for the night

7   Total time asleep for the night

8   Sleep efficiency for the night

9   How would you rate your quality   Great   Good   Fair   Poor
of sleep for the night?

10   How long did you doze or nap
during the day yesterday?

11   Additional Notes

NOTE FROM A THERAPIST

You made it through your first week of sleep restriction! Now you'll have an opportunity to assess and
adjust your sleep goals.

Calculate Your
Goals for Week III

Now that you've implemented your bedtime and wake time goals for a week, you can determine whether you should consider any adjustments to your sleep schedule.

1   CALCULATE YOUR AVERAGE SLEEP EFFICIENCY
      FOR THE PAST WEEK

WEEK 2: AVERAGE SLEEP EFFICIENCY									
NIGHT	1	2	3	4	5	6	7	TOTAL	AVERAGE (TOTAL ÷ 7)
SLEEP EFFICIENCY									

2   ADJUST YOUR ALLOWABLE TIME IN BED,
      BEDTIME, AND WAKE TIME

If your sleep efficiency was at least 85%, you felt "Good" most days this past week, and you didn't nap most days, maintain your Allowable Time in Bed.

If your sleep efficiency was at least 85%, but you felt especially drowsy or fatigued during the day, or you took several naps, increase your Allowable Time in Bed by 15 minutes.

If your sleep efficiency was less than 85%, or you felt especially drowsy or fatigued during the day, or you took several naps, maintain your Allowable Time in Bed.

3   SET AND COMMIT TO YOUR NEW WAKE TIME
      AND BEDTIME

WAKE TIME		
ALLOWABLE TIME IN BED	MAINTAIN ALLOWABLE TIME IN BED	INCREASE YOUR ALLOWABLE TIME IN BED BY 15 MINUTES
BEDTIME		

WEEK III:
Stimulus Control

Note From a Therapist

As much as sleep is an innate, daily behavior, it's also a learned one. Unwittingly, we make associations with our environments and actions around sleep.

People with sleep issues may spend hours in bed tossing and turning, watching the clock, reading, or other activities, desperately trying to fall asleep. They reason, "I need to be in bed to get as much sleep as I can." While well-intentioned, this teaches the brain and body to associate the bed as a place to do anything—not just sleep.

Stimulus control within CBT-I refers to the deliberate linking of "bed" with "sleep." If your body learns, "when I lie down, I'm sleeping," then you'll be much better in control of when you fall asleep. In order to establish that association, you want to do the following things:

- Only go to bed when you're drowsy and ready to sleep

- Only use your bed for sleeping (and sex)

- Get out of bed if you haven't fallen asleep in 15 minutes—do something unstimulating and low energy until you feel drowsy before going back to bed

- Avoid taking naps—this disrupts your nighttime sleep

- Make your clock dim or turn over your phone to reduce time spent staring at the clock

Doing these things may be difficult and feel like they are interrupting the sleep you "could be getting," but will strengthen your sleep habits and let you sleep when you want to. For this next week, intentionally incorporate the practices above and take note of how each day feels in your sleep log, keeping in mind that the goal is to increase your sleep drive for better sleep.

WEEK III:
Your Sleep Log Entries

	WEEKLY SLEEP GOAL
WAKE TIME	
BEDTIME	

1   What time did you get into bed?

. . . .

2   What time did you fall asleep?

. . . .

3   How long were you up in the
        middle of the night?

. . . .

4   What time did you finally wake up?

. . . .

5   What time did you finally get out
        of bed?

. . . .

6   Total time in bed for the night

. . . .

7   Total time asleep for the night

. . . .

8   Sleep efficiency for the night

. . . .

9   How would you rate your quality   Great   Good   Fair   Poor
        of sleep for the night?

. . . .

10   How long did you doze or nap
        during the day yesterday?

. . . .

11   Additional Notes

. . . .

. . . .

. . . .

. . . .

. . . .

. . . .

NOTE FROM A THERAPIST

Stimulus control is a way to reduce the things that
keep you up at night. Consider: what gets in the
way of your sleep?

1	What time did you get into bed?
2	What time did you fall asleep?
3	How long were you up in the middle of the night?
4	What time did you finally wake up?
5	What time did you finally get out of bed?
6	Total time in bed for the night
7	Total time asleep for the night
8	Sleep efficiency for the night
9	How would you rate your quality of sleep for the night?	Great	Good	Fair	Poor
10	How long did you doze or nap during the day yesterday?
11	Additional Notes

NOTE FROM A THERAPIST

If you are in the habit of working or watching TV
in bed, brainstorm other places for this—even if it's
the bedroom floor.

1   What time did you get into bed?

2   What time did you fall asleep?

3   How long were you up in the
         middle of the night?

4   What time did you finally wake up?

5   What time did you finally get out
         of bed?

6   Total time in bed for the night

7   Total time asleep for the night

8   Sleep efficiency for the night

9   How would you rate your quality   Great   Good   Fair   Poor
         of sleep for the night?

10   How long did you doze or nap
         during the day yesterday?

11   Additional Notes

NOTE FROM A THERAPIST

Create a cozy and comfortable place to relax in
another part of your house with pillows, blankets,
and warm lighting.

1   What time did you get into bed?

2   What time did you fall asleep?

3   How long were you up in the
            middle of the night?

4   What time did you finally wake up?

5   What time did you finally get out
            of bed?

6   Total time in bed for the night

7   Total time asleep for the night

8   Sleep efficiency for the night

9   How would you rate your quality   Great   Good   Fair   Poor
            of sleep for the night?

10   How long did you doze or nap
            during the day yesterday?

11   Additional Notes

NOTE FROM A THERAPIST

If you're not sure what to do while you're awake in
the middle of the night, reference Appendix A for
some calming ideas.

1   What time did you get into bed?

2   What time did you fall asleep?

3   How long were you up in the
middle of the night?

4   What time did you finally wake up?

5   What time did you finally get out
of bed?

6   Total time in bed for the night

7   Total time asleep for the night

8   Sleep efficiency for the night

9   How would you rate your quality   Great   Good   Fair   Poor
of sleep for the night?

10   How long did you doze or nap
during the day yesterday?

11   Additional Notes

NOTE FROM A THERAPIST

If you're having trouble winding down for bed, try
focusing your attention to your breath.

1   What time did you get into bed?

2   What time did you fall asleep?

3   How long were you up in the
           middle of the night?

4   What time did you finally wake up?

5   What time did you finally get out
           of bed?

6   Total time in bed for the night

7   Total time asleep for the night

8   Sleep efficiency for the night

9   How would you rate your quality   Great   Good   Fair   Poor
           of sleep for the night?

10   How long did you doze or nap
           during the day yesterday?

11   Additional Notes

NOTE FROM A THERAPIST

What are the biggest factors that interfere with
your "bed equals sleep" association?

1   What time did you get into bed?

2   What time did you fall asleep?

3   How long were you up in the middle of the night?

4   What time did you finally wake up?

5   What time did you finally get out of bed?

6   Total time in bed for the night

7   Total time asleep for the night

8   Sleep efficiency for the night

9   How would you rate your quality of sleep for the night?   Great   Good   Fair   Poor

10   How long did you doze or nap during the day yesterday?

11   Additional Notes

NOTE FROM A THERAPIST

Try to keep your phone in the other room.
When the alarm goes off, it will force you to
get up—and wake up.

Calculate Your
Goals for Week IV

1   CALCULATE YOUR AVERAGE SLEEP EFFICIENCY FOR THE PAST WEEK

WEEK 3: AVERAGE SLEEP EFFICIENCY									
NIGHT	1	2	3	4	5	6	7	TOTAL	AVERAGE (TOTAL ÷ 7)
SLEEP EFFICIENCY									

2   ADJUST YOUR ALLOWABLE TIME IN BED, BEDTIME, AND WAKE TIME

If your sleep efficiency was at least 85%, you felt "Good" most days this past week, and you didn't nap most days, maintain your Allowable Time in Bed.

If your sleep efficiency was at least 85%, but you felt especially drowsy or fatigued during the day, or you took several naps, increase your Allowable Time in Bed by 15 minutes.

If your sleep efficiency was less than 85%, or you felt especially drowsy or fatigued during the day, or you took several naps, maintain your Allowable Time in Bed.

3   SET AND COMMIT TO YOUR NEW WAKE TIME AND BEDTIME

WAKE TIME		
ALLOWABLE TIME IN BED	MAINTAIN ALLOWABLE TIME IN BED	INCREASE YOUR ALLOWABLE TIME IN BED BY 15 MINUTES
BEDTIME		

WEEK IV:
Sleep Hygiene

Note From a Therapist

Sleep hygiene refers to all of the helpful things you can do to improve the quality and quantity of your sleep. Sleep hygiene is important for everyone, even those with good quality sleep, to practice. It's even more important for those with insomnia or other sleep problems to incorporate into their routines. For this next week, try incorporating 1–3 of the below practices. Do the same set of practices for several nights, as it can take some time to see an effect. Use the "Additional Notes" to log the kind of effect you notice on your sleep throughout the week.

• Unwind for 1 hour before bedtime

Help your brain transition from the stimulation of the day by establishing a consistent wind-down routine. This can include disconnecting from your screens, reading a light book, doing relaxation exercises, and getting ready for bed.

• Avoid caffeine after noon

Caffeine stays in your system even 12 hours after you consume it, past when you feel its active effects. Have your morning coffee or tea, and then try going for walks, doing jumping jacks, or taking a mental break to keep you going through the afternoon.

• Limit alcohol in the evening, and avoid one hour before bed

While alcohol can be helpful for falling asleep, it actually makes you sleep lighter and wake more often during the night. Give your body the chance to fully process any alcohol you have before going to bed—a good rule of thumb is one hour per drink.

- Avoid nicotine before bed

People mistakenly believe that smoking helps us relax. This is partially true. Nicotine can have a relaxing effect as it enters our system, but it's actually a stimulant. As it builds in our system, it acts like caffeine and gets us wired.

- Exercise during the day

Regular exercise (in whatever form suits you) has been shown to improve mood and improve sleep quality. Exercise can help you feel more fatigued, fall asleep faster, and sleep more deeply. However, limit exercise in the evening, since endorphins and the stimulating effects of exercise can interfere with sleep as well.

- Maintain a bedroom environment conducive to sleep

Create a dark, quiet, and cool environment to sleep in. Consider using blackout shades, eye masks, earplugs, white noise machines, and setting the temperature within the 60's.

- Take a warm bath

A warm bath or shower can loosen your muscles, helping you relax before bed. The drop in body temperature when you get out can also help signal your body for sleep.

WEEK IV:
Your Sleep Log Entries

WEEKLY SLEEP GOAL	
WAKE TIME	
BEDTIME	

1   What time did you get into bed?

2   What time did you fall asleep?

3   How long were you up in the
           middle of the night?

4   What time did you finally wake up?

5   What time did you finally get out
           of bed?

6   Total time in bed for the night

7   Total time asleep for the night

8   Sleep efficiency for the night

9   How would you rate your quality   Great   Good   Fair   Poor
           of sleep for the night?

10   How long did you doze or nap
           during the day yesterday?

11   Additional Notes

NOTE FROM A THERAPIST

Take stock of your wind-down routine. Does it
help you relax before bed? If you don't have one,
consider putting one in place.

1   What time did you get into bed?

2   What time did you fall asleep?

3   How long were you up in the
     middle of the night?

4   What time did you finally wake up?

5   What time did you finally get out
     of bed?

6   Total time in bed for the night

7   Total time asleep for the night

8   Sleep efficiency for the night

9   How would you rate your quality   Great   Good   Fair   Poor
     of sleep for the night?

10   How long did you doze or nap
     during the day yesterday?

11   Additional Notes

NOTE FROM A THERAPIST

Take a moment to survey your sleep environment.
Is it cool, dark, and comfortable?

1   What time did you get into bed?

2   What time did you fall asleep?

3   How long were you up in the
           middle of the night?

4   What time did you finally wake up?

5   What time did you finally get out
           of bed?

6   Total time in bed for the night

7   Total time asleep for the night

8   Sleep efficiency for the night

9   How would you rate your quality   Great   Good   Fair   Poor
           of sleep for the night?

10   How long did you doze or nap
           during the day yesterday?

11   Additional Notes

NOTE FROM A THERAPIST

Be aware of daytime behaviors that interfere
with sleep, like drinking coffee or exercising late
in the day.

1   What time did you get into bed?

2   What time did you fall asleep?

3   How long were you up in the
middle of the night?

4   What time did you finally wake up?

5   What time did you finally get out
of bed?

6   Total time in bed for the night

7   Total time asleep for the night

8   Sleep efficiency for the night

9   How would you rate your quality   Great   Good   Fair   Poor
of sleep for the night?

10   How long did you doze or nap
during the day yesterday?

11   Additional Notes

NOTE FROM A THERAPIST

Brainstorm alternatives to sleep-interfering behaviors. For example, try drinking decaf tea instead of coffee in the afternoon.

1   What time did you get into bed?

. . . .

2   What time did you fall asleep?

. . . .

3   How long were you up in the
         middle of the night?

. . . .

4   What time did you finally wake up?

. . . .

5   What time did you finally get out
         of bed?

. . . .

6   Total time in bed for the night

. . . .

7   Total time asleep for the night

. . . .

8   Sleep efficiency for the night

. . . .

9   How would you rate your quality   Great   Good   Fair   Poor
         of sleep for the night?

. . . .

10   How long did you doze or nap
         during the day yesterday?

. . . .

11   Additional Notes

. . . .

. . . .

. . . .

. . . .

. . . .

. . . .

NOTE FROM A THERAPIST

Sleep supports your lifestyle just as your lifestyle
supports your sleep. Keep up the progress.

1   What time did you get into bed?

2   What time did you fall asleep?

3   How long were you up in the middle of the night?

4   What time did you finally wake up?

5   What time did you finally get out of bed?

6   Total time in bed for the night

7   Total time asleep for the night

8   Sleep efficiency for the night

9   How would you rate your quality of sleep for the night?   Great   Good   Fair   Poor

10   How long did you doze or nap during the day yesterday?

11   Additional Notes

NOTE FROM A THERAPIST

Commit to sleep hygiene changes that feel realistic
and sustainable.

1   What time did you get into bed?

2   What time did you fall asleep?

3   How long were you up in the middle of the night?

4   What time did you finally wake up?

5   What time did you finally get out of bed?

6   Total time in bed for the night

7   Total time asleep for the night

8   Sleep efficiency for the night

9   How would you rate your quality of sleep for the night?   Great   Good   Fair   Poor

10   How long did you doze or nap during the day yesterday?

11   Additional Notes

NOTE FROM A THERAPIST

Do your best to implement a change for several nights over the course of the week to notice differences in your sleep.

Calculate Your
Goals for Week V

1   CALCULATE YOUR AVERAGE SLEEP EFFICIENCY FOR THE PAST WEEK

WEEK 4: AVERAGE SLEEP EFFICIENCY									
NIGHT	1	2	3	4	5	6	7	TOTAL	AVERAGE (TOTAL ÷ 7)
SLEEP EFFICIENCY									

2   ADJUST YOUR ALLOWABLE TIME IN BED, BEDTIME, AND WAKE TIME

If your sleep efficiency was at least 85%, you felt "Good" most days this past week, and you didn't nap most days, maintain your Allowable Time in Bed.

If your sleep efficiency was at least 85%, but you felt especially drowsy or fatigued during the day, or you took several naps, increase your Allowable Time in Bed by 15 minutes.

If your sleep efficiency was less than 85%, or you felt especially drowsy or fatigued during the day, or you took several naps, maintain your Allowable Time in Bed.

3   SET AND COMMIT TO YOUR NEW WAKE TIME AND BEDTIME

WAKE TIME		
ALLOWABLE TIME IN BED	MAINTAIN ALLOWABLE TIME IN BED	INCREASE YOUR ALLOWABLE TIME IN BED BY 15 MINUTES
BEDTIME		

WEEK V:
Cognitive Reframing

Note From a Therapist

People with insomnia and other sleep difficulties tend to develop specific, unhelpful thoughts and beliefs like, "There's nothing I can do about my sleep," or, "I just need to try harder to sleep." These thoughts can make us feel like we don't have any control over our sleep, when in actuality, we can improve it.

If you find yourself thinking any of the above—or having other rigid beliefs about sleep—try what psychologists call "Cognitive Reframing" or "Cognitive Restructuring." In short, this exercise asks you to identify the unhelpful thought and come up with an alternative thought that is more balanced with the likelihood of that happening versus other possibilities.

Follow the instructions:

NAME THE THOUGHT

Example: "If I don't get 8 hours of sleep, my day will be ruined."

QUESTION THE THOUGHT

Ask yourself: if I take a step back, how true is that thought? How much of my thought is an exaggeration? What parts of my thought are accurate and true? What parts of my thought are an exaggeration or fear? What can I control about the situation that brings on this thought?

REFRAME THE THOUGHT

Come up with a more accurate, balanced thought by integrating the answers to the questions above into a new thought.

Example: "I don't typically get 8 hours of sleep. So if I don't get 8 hours of sleep tonight, I'll be tired. But I can make the most of my energy in the morning by prioritizing important tasks for that time."

This upcoming week, take note of how you were able to implement Cognitive Reframing; feel free to jot down the unhelpful thought, and the more balanced thought you arrived at. As you write down your unhelpful and balanced thoughts, notice patterns that can help remind you of how you've been able to poke holes in your worries.

WEEK V:
Your Sleep Log Entries

WEEKLY SLEEP GOAL	
WAKE TIME	
BEDTIME	

1   What time did you get into bed?

2   What time did you fall asleep?

3   How long were you up in the
               middle of the night?

4   What time did you finally wake up?

5   What time did you finally get out
               of bed?

6   Total time in bed for the night

7   Total time asleep for the night

8   Sleep efficiency for the night

9   How would you rate your quality   Great   Good   Fair   Poor
               of sleep for the night?

10   How long did you doze or nap
               during the day yesterday?

11   Additional Notes

NOTE FROM A THERAPIST

If you're having trouble identifying thoughts that
interfere with your sleep, start with distressing
emotions that come up.

1   What time did you get into bed?

2   What time did you fall asleep?

3   How long were you up in the
         middle of the night?

4   What time did you finally wake up?

5   What time did you finally get out
         of bed?

6   Total time in bed for the night

7   Total time asleep for the night

8   Sleep efficiency for the night

9   How would you rate your quality   Great   Good   Fair   Poor
         of sleep for the night?

10   How long did you doze or nap
         during the day yesterday?

11   Additional Notes

NOTE FROM A THERAPIST

When practicing cognitive reframing, remember
to frame the anxiety-inducing thought so it's more
realistic and balanced.

1   What time did you get into bed?

2   What time did you fall asleep?

3   How long were you up in the middle of the night?

4   What time did you finally wake up?

5   What time did you finally get out of bed?

6   Total time in bed for the night

7   Total time asleep for the night

8   Sleep efficiency for the night

9   How would you rate your quality of sleep for the night?   Great   Good   Fair   Poor

10   How long did you doze or nap during the day yesterday?

11   Additional Notes

NOTE FROM A THERAPIST

Notice if you plan for the next day as you're winding down. Instead, try reserving time to do mental housekeeping during the day.

1　　　What time did you get into bed?

2　　　What time did you fall asleep?

3　　　How long were you up in the
　　　middle of the night?

4　　　What time did you finally wake up?

5　　　What time did you finally get out
　　　of bed?

6　　　Total time in bed for the night

7　　　Total time asleep for the night

8　　　Sleep efficiency for the night

9　　　How would you rate your quality　　Great　　Good　　Fair　　Poor
　　　of sleep for the night?

10　　How long did you doze or nap
　　　during the day yesterday?

11　　Additional Notes

NOTE FROM A THERAPIST

Be fair to yourself when practicing cognitive
reframing–the goal is to find balance in your
thoughts.

1   What time did you get into bed?

2   What time did you fall asleep?

3   How long were you up in the middle of the night?

4   What time did you finally wake up?

5   What time did you finally get out of bed?

6   Total time in bed for the night

7   Total time asleep for the night

8   Sleep efficiency for the night

9   How would you rate your quality of sleep for the night?   Great   Good   Fair   Poor

10   How long did you doze or nap during the day yesterday?

11   Additional Notes

NOTE FROM A THERAPIST

When you're reframing a thought, it can be helpful to remember how we've navigated similar situations in the past.

1   What time did you get into bed?

2   What time did you fall asleep?

3   How long were you up in the
         middle of the night?

4   What time did you finally wake up?

5   What time did you finally get out
         of bed?

6   Total time in bed for the night

7   Total time asleep for the night

8   Sleep efficiency for the night

9   How would you rate your quality   Great   Good   Fair   Poor
         of sleep for the night?

10   How long did you doze or nap
         during the day yesterday?

11   Additional Notes

NOTE FROM A THERAPIST

Try your best to present a balanced viewpoint in
your thoughts, recognizing both what you may
struggle with and what you do well.

1   What time did you get into bed?

2   What time did you fall asleep?

3   How long were you up in the
             middle of the night?

4   What time did you finally wake up?

5   What time did you finally get out
             of bed?

6   Total time in bed for the night

7   Total time asleep for the night

8   Sleep efficiency for the night

9   How would you rate your quality   Great   Good   Fair   Poor
             of sleep for the night?

10   How long did you doze or nap
             during the day yesterday?

11   Additional Notes

NOTE FROM A THERAPIST

Remember to practice patience and self-com-
passion around your sleep difficulties. We're
committed to progress, not perfection.

Calculate Your Goals for Week VI

1   CALCULATE YOUR AVERAGE SLEEP EFFICIENCY FOR THE PAST WEEK

WEEK 5: AVERAGE SLEEP EFFICIENCY								
NIGHT	1	2	3	4	5	6	7	TOTAL	AVERAGE (TOTAL ÷ 7)
SLEEP EFFICIENCY								

2   ADJUST YOUR ALLOWABLE TIME IN BED, BEDTIME, AND WAKE TIME

If your sleep efficiency was at least 85%, you felt "Good" most days this past week, and you didn't nap most days, maintain your Allowable Time in Bed.

If your sleep efficiency was at least 85%, but you felt especially drowsy or fatigued during the day, or you took several naps, increase your Allowable Time in Bed by 15 minutes.

If your sleep efficiency was less than 85%, or you felt especially drowsy or fatigued during the day, or you took several naps, maintain your Allowable Time in Bed.

3   SET AND COMMIT TO YOUR NEW WAKE TIME AND BEDTIME

WAKE TIME		
ALLOWABLE TIME IN BED	MAINTAIN ALLOWABLE TIME IN BED	INCREASE YOUR ALLOWABLE TIME IN BED BY 15 MINUTES
BEDTIME		

WEEK VI:
Relapse Prevention

Note From
a Therapist

You've made it nearly to the end. Take time to reflect, take stock, and plan for any future hiccups. This plan is called "Relapse Prevention." Having a plan in place to recognize and respond to emerging issues prevents you from falling back into the sleep struggles you were in before.

As you design your plan, it's helpful to consider the following:

- How has your sleep changed?

- What CBT-I principles from this book were most helpful to you?

- What systems or supports can you put in place to maintain them?

In the future, if you notice yourself lying awake in the middle of the night, reflect on whether there is something affecting your sleep—such as stress, illness, changes in routine, or even positive events. Identifying the reason can help things feel more manageable.

If you're noticing yourself having sleep trouble frequently for more than a couple weeks, it may be time to be more proactive in utilizing your sleep skills. If your sleep problems persist for more than three months or worsen to the extent that they are affecting your job or relationships, consider reaching out to your primary care physician or a sleep expert.

Having a plan in place to maintain your new behaviors, knowing how to recognize if sleep is developing into an issue again, and identifying what is most effective for you will prepare you for handling future sleep trouble.

WEEK VI:
Your Sleep Log Entries

	WEEKLY SLEEP GOAL
WAKE TIME	
BEDTIME	

1   What time did you get into bed?

2   What time did you fall asleep?

3   How long were you up in the
         middle of the night?

4   What time did you finally wake up?

5   What time did you finally get out
         of bed?

6   Total time in bed for the night

7   Total time asleep for the night

8   Sleep efficiency for the night

9   How would you rate your quality   Great   Good   Fair   Poor
         of sleep for the night?

10   How long did you doze or nap
         during the day yesterday?

11   Additional Notes

NOTE FROM A THERAPIST

Even if you did not meet your goals every night,
take a moment to recognize how your overall sleep
may be improving.

1   What time did you get into bed?

. . . .

2   What time did you fall asleep?

. . . .

3   How long were you up in the
         middle of the night?

. . . .

4   What time did you finally wake up?

. . . .

5   What time did you finally get out
         of bed?

. . . .

6   Total time in bed for the night

. . . .

7   Total time asleep for the night

. . . .

8   Sleep efficiency for the night

. . . .

9   How would you rate your quality   Great   Good   Fair   Poor
         of sleep for the night?

. . . .

10   How long did you doze or nap
         during the day yesterday?

. . . .

11   Additional Notes

. . . .

. . . .

. . . .

. . . .

. . . .

NOTE FROM A THERAPIST

Identify what changes you implemented into your
daily routine that supported your sleep.

1   What time did you get into bed?

2   What time did you fall asleep?

3   How long were you up in the middle of the night?

4   What time did you finally wake up?

5   What time did you finally get out of bed?

6   Total time in bed for the night

7   Total time asleep for the night

8   Sleep efficiency for the night

9   How would you rate your quality of sleep for the night?   Great   Good   Fair   Poor

10   How long did you doze or nap during the day yesterday?

11   Additional Notes

NOTE FROM A THERAPIST

Consider what has felt easier or more manageable
since you started working on your sleep.

1   What time did you get into bed?

2   What time did you fall asleep?

3   How long were you up in the
           middle of the night?

4   What time did you finally wake up?

5   What time did you finally get out
           of bed?

6   Total time in bed for the night

7   Total time asleep for the night

8   Sleep efficiency for the night

9   How would you rate your quality   Great   Good   Fair   Poor
           of sleep for the night?

10   How long did you doze or nap
           during the day yesterday?

11   Additional Notes

NOTE FROM A THERAPIST

Take stock of your progress. Are you getting more
sleep? More importantly, do you feel better rested
during the day?

1   What time did you get into bed?

2   What time did you fall asleep?

3   How long were you up in the
        middle of the night?

4   What time did you finally wake up?

5   What time did you finally get out
        of bed?

6   Total time in bed for the night

7   Total time asleep for the night

8   Sleep efficiency for the night

9   How would you rate your quality   Great   Good   Fair   Poor
        of sleep for the night?

10   How long did you doze or nap
        during the day yesterday?

11   Additional Notes

NOTE FROM A THERAPIST

Identify what factors helped you meet your goal
times in the past weeks, and how you might intentionally implement them.

1   What time did you get into bed?

2   What time did you fall asleep?

3   How long were you up in the middle of the night?

4   What time did you finally wake up?

5   What time did you finally get out of bed?

6   Total time in bed for the night

7   Total time asleep for the night

8   Sleep efficiency for the night

9   How would you rate your quality of sleep for the night?   Great   Good   Fair   Poor

10   How long did you doze or nap during the day yesterday?

11   Additional Notes

NOTE FROM A THERAPIST

Sleep needs and sleep quality can change over time.
A few nights of sleep trouble does not mean you're
back to square one.

1   What time did you get into bed?

2   What time did you fall asleep?

3   How long were you up in the middle of the night?

4   What time did you finally wake up?

5   What time did you finally get out of bed?

6   Total time in bed for the night

7   Total time asleep for the night

8   Sleep efficiency for the night

9   How would you rate your quality of sleep for the night?   Great   Good   Fair   Poor

10   How long did you doze or nap during the day yesterday?

11   Additional Notes

NOTE FROM A THERAPIST

Even though your journal entries are done,
this journal is here for you. Come back as often
as you need.

Final Note From
a Therapist

Congratulations! You've completed the program. After logging, calculating, reflecting, and adjusting, you learned about your sleep behavior and have hopefully found some respite under the covers. As you know, sleep can be tricky and many of the factors that impact us, (such as age, hormones, stress, medication, life transitions), are beyond our control. The key is to focus on what we can control, like how the brain relates to its environment and to sleep.

Remember—"bed = sleep." Consider the best practices you've learned throughout these six weeks:

- Maintain a consistent sleep schedule–even on weekends.

- Only go to bed when you're drowsy and ready to sleep.

- Use your bed only for sleep (and sex).

- If you haven't fallen asleep in fifteen minutes, get out of bed and do something light and boring until you feel drowsy.

- Avoid naps as much as possible.

- Give your brain and body time to transition and prepare for sleep.

- Reframe unhelpful thoughts about sleep.

You now have some effective tools and personalized data to get the rest you deserve. Keep in mind that these skills are mastered over time. They're meant to both improve your sleep and help to maintain it. So, continue practicing them. You don't have to get them right every night, but keep at it. The effort and consistency will pay off. And of course, refer back to this book as much as you'd like.

A   Tips for When You're Having Trouble Sleeping

In addition to all of the negative effects of sleep loss, sleep trouble can be frustrating. We've included suggestions to ease your in-the-moment anxiety and get you to a drowsier state quickly.

STEP ONE: GET OUT OF BED

The longer you stay in bed not sleeping, the more your brain and body will associate your bed with anything but sleep. Move elsewhere–to a chair, a couch, the floor, or even to a standing position.

STEP TWO: ALLOW YOURSELF TO RELAX

Take deep breaths, massage your neck, and roll your shoulders. If disheartening thoughts are creeping into your mind such as, "I'm never going to get to sleep tonight," envision a Stop sign that keeps your thoughts from moving. These thoughts will only cause more distress, which makes it harder to sleep.

STEP THREE: DO MUNDANE, MONOTONOUS TASKS

Do mundane, monotonous tasks to pass the time until you feel drowsy enough to go to bed.

A few ideas to get you started:

- Take a slow walk around your house.
- Eat a light snack (nothing too flavorful) or drink a cup of hot milk or herbal tea.
- Read a nonfiction book or listen to a podcast. Choose something that isn't too stimulating (something you can easily put down).
- Complete a few mundane chores such as folding laundry, dusting, or organizing your junk drawer.
- Listen to some guided mindfulness exercises, or practice breathing exercises (but avoid using your phone).

Try not to:

- Stare at your alarm clock.
- Reach for your phone and start reading your email, browsing websites, or checking social media.
- Turn on your TV and start watching your favorite movie or TV show.

B   Frequently Asked Questions

Q: *Do I actually need to log every item every night? What if I just approximate it at the end of the week?*

A: Doing the logging can be time consuming, but because each individual's sleep schedule and needs are unique, you need to gather your personal "data." That data comes from your sleep logs. On an individual log, you can roughly approximate the times (rounding in 5-15 minute increments is fine). Within a set of seven sleep logs, complete at least five to get a good group to average from. If you forgot to do your sleep log more than two mornings in a week, push back when you adjust your sleep schedule to get five nights' worth of logs.

Q: *What's the difference between "sleep efficiency" and "sleep drive"?*

A: Sleep drive refers to the body's need and desire for sleep. Based on your previous night's sleep and your circadian rhythm, adenosine builds up over the day to make you feel fatigued and ready for bed. Sleep efficiency refers to how much of the time in bed you spent actually sleeping. If you spent 10 hours in bed, but were only asleep for 5, then you'd have 50% sleep efficiency.

Q: *I just started Week 2 and I'm so exhausted! What should I do?*

A: Feeling particularly tired and getting less sleep initially is part of CBT-I. As you consolidate your sleep, it'll seem as though you're staying up way later, or waking up way earlier. As your sleep efficiency improves, you'll be able to extend your time in bed to allow for more sleep. Right now, unless you feel like you're going to fall asleep involuntarily, try to maintain your wake and bedtimes and avoid naps. If you do think you're at risk for falling asleep, especially while doing a high risk activity like driving, it's okay to take a brief 10-20 minute nap during the day. The earlier the nap, the better.

Q: *What if I'm not totally sure about the time I fell asleep, or how long I was awake during the night?*

A: Do your best to estimate these times. It's okay to guess in up to 15 minute increments. As much as we want good data, we also don't want you to be staring at your clock in bed or focusing too much on accuracy at the expense of sleep.

Q: *I often feel most productive at night and work right up until bedtime. What should I do?*

A: See if you can set a wake and bed time that is realistic, takes into account your typical schedule, and allows for adequate wind-down time. You might consider setting bed time a little later, and scheduling your wake time accordingly.

Q: *I feel too tired during the day to get my work done. Can I change my sleep schedule?*

A: That depends on your sleep efficiency. If you're hitting at least 85% sleep efficiency, then the following week, you can add 15 minutes to your Allowable Time in Bed. However, unless you're falling asleep on your feet, you should continue with your planned sleep schedule.

Q: *Will I ever get to schedule sleep for more than just a few hours?*

A: Yes! As your sleep becomes more efficient, you'll be able to increase the amount of time you spend in bed until you reach the point where you're not tired during the day. This may not happen within the context of these six weeks, but the principles being practiced here will continue to inform how you adjust your sleep schedule.

C   Fundamentals of Self-Care

Sleep is not a function of the body that works in isolation. It impacts, and is impacted by your other daily habits and fundamentals of self-care. Making sure that these other factors are well taken care of can improve your sleep—without even feeling like you're working on sleep.

NUTRITION

Maintaining your body's nutritional needs is essential for regulating your sense of fatigue and energy levels.

Example: Try to eat throughout the day (three or more snacks or meals is a good start), doing your best to include a variety of food groups.

EXERCISE

Movement releases endorphins, which in turn relieves stress and gets your body up and going during the day, instead of at night when you're trying to calm down.

Example: Try to incorporate movement during the day that gets your heart rate up, like climbing stairs, or dancing.

SUBSTANCE USE

Caffeine, alcohol, cannabis, and other substances can disrupt your body's natural regulating systems. Stimulants (like caffeine or nicotine) can affect your body long after you feel its effects, and depressants (such as alcohol) can interfere with your sleep quality.

Example: A way to limit substances is to buy less to decrease its availability, and to put it in inconvenient places (e.g. above the fridge, or in the back of a closet) to make it harder to access.

PHYSICAL HEALTH

Illnesses, chronic issues, and hormonal imbalances can take a toll on your sleep by making it uncomfortable to lie down, or inducing chronic bodily fatigue.

Example: Make regular check-ups a priority, and be sure to speak to your doctor about sleep issues.

MINDFULNESS

Practicing mindfulness throughout the day and particularly at night can help calm the system, manage emotions, and build present-moment awareness.

Example: Take a few deep breaths, focusing on the sensations in your body when you inhale, and warmth of the air when you exhale.

References

[1] Smith, M. T., Perlis, M. L., Park, A., Smith, M. S., Pennington, J., Giles, D. E., & Buysse, D. J. (2002). Comparative meta-analysis of pharmacotherapy and behavior therapy for persistent insomnia. The American journal of psychiatry, 159(1), 5–11. ▸ https://doi.org/10.1176/appi.ajp.159.1.5

[2] Mitchell, M. D., Gehrman, P., Perlis, M., & Umscheid, C. A. (2012). Comparative effectiveness of cognitive behavioral therapy for insomnia: a systematic review. BMC family practice, 13, 40. ▸ https://doi.org/10.1186/1471-2296-13-40

[3] FAQs for cognitive behavioral therapy for insomnia (CBT-I). (n.d.). Center for Deployment Psychology. ▸ https://deploymentpsych.org/content/faqs-cognitive-behavioral-therapy-insomnia-cbt-i

[4] Insomnia overview: Epidemiology, pathophysiology, diagnosis and monitoring, and Nonpharmacologic therapy. (2020, April 13). AJMC. ▸ https://doi.org/10.37765/ajmc.2020.42769

[5] O'Brien, E. M., & Boland, E. M. (2020). CBT-I is an efficacious, first-line treatment for insomnia: Where we need to go from here. A commentary on the application of Tolin's criteria to cognitive behavioral therapy for insomnia. Clinical Psychology: Science and Practice, 27(4). ▸ https://doi.org/10.1111/cpsp.12370

[6] 'Wild nights' offers a history of sleep (and sleeplessness) (Published 2017). (2017, March 1). The New York Times - Breaking News, US News, World News and Videos. ▸ https://www.nytimes.com/2017/03/01/books/wild-nights-benjamin-reiss.html

[7] Walker, M. P., & van der Helm, E. (2009). Overnight therapy? The role of sleep in emotional brain processing. Psychological bulletin, 135(5), 731–748. ▸ https://doi.org/10.1037/a0016570

[8] Goldstein, A. N., & Walker, M. P. (2014). The role of sleep in emotional brain function. Annual review of clinical psychology, 10, 679–708. ▸ https://doi.org/10.1146/annurev-clinpsy-032813-153716

[9] Cappuccio, F. P., D'Elia, L., Strazzullo, P., & Miller, M. A. (2010). Sleep duration and all-cause mortality: a systematic review and meta-analysis of prospective studies. Sleep, 33(5), 585–592. ▸ https://doi.org/10.1093/sleep/33.5.585

[10] Nagai, M., Hoshide, S., & Kario, K. (2010). Sleep duration as a risk factor for cardiovascular disease- a review of the recent literature. Current cardiology reviews, 6(1), 54–61. ▸ https://doi.org/10.2174/157340310790231635

[11] Wolk, R., Gami, A. S., Garcia-Touchard, A., & Somers, V. K. (2005). Sleep and cardiovascular disease. Current problems in cardiology, 30(12), 625–662. ▸ https://doi.org/10.1016/j.cpcardiol.2005.07.002

[12] Khurshid K. A. (2018). Comorbid Insomnia and Psychiatric Disorders: An Update. Innovations in clinical neuroscience, 15(3-4), 28–32.

[13] Taylor, D. J., Mallory, L. J., Lichstein, K. L., Durrence, H. H., Riedel, B. W., & Bush, A. J. (2007). Comorbidity of chronic insomnia with medical problems. Sleep, 30(2), 213–218. ▸ *https://doi.org/10.1093/sleep/30.2.213*

[14] The effects of seasons and weather on sleep patterns measured through longitudinal multimodal sensing. (2021, April 28). npj Digital Medicine.
▸ *https://www.nature.com/articles/s41746-021-00435-2*